— GET TO THE —
ROOT

A WOMAN'S GUIDE TO
Emotional Healing

RACHEL LOGAN, LCSW

GET TO THE ROOT
A Woman's Guide To Emotional Healing

Rachel L. Logan, LCSW
Shiloh, IL
www.gettotherootcounseling.com
Rachel@gettotherootcounseling.com
618-310-0422

ISBN 978-1-949826-32-6
Printed in the USA.
All rights reserved

Published by: EAGLES GLOBAL BOOKS | Frisco, Texas
In conjunction with the 2021 Eagles Authors Course
Cover & interior designed by DestinedToPublish.com

Table of Contents

Get to the Root!

Introduction

A majority of people have experienced hardships, trauma, abuse, or hurt and just kept living. People do not stop to assess how it has impacted them. In my culture and family, I was trained to move on from pain instead of processing it. Pain is often swept under the rug and ignored. At other times, we become so accepting of discomfort that we start to believe it is a part of our lives. The truth is: *Living in a constant state of discomfort should not be your reality.*

Have you ever been so busy that you did not know that you hurt yourself? You know, you are whipping up a good meal and you accidentally cut your finger, and you happen to look down to see that you are bleeding. (By the way, that really happened to me.) Athletes experience this often. For instance, football players tackle each other repeatedly and sprint up and down the field for the duration of the game. They jump over players, extend their arms, tumble to the ground. In all of kinds of weather conditions, for four long quarters, players aim to have the winning score. They are oblivious to the condition of their body. They are so occupied that they do not realize they scuffed their knee or hurt their shoulders. They keep playing the game even if their head is pounding. They do not stop moving until the end of the game. When football players get to the locker room and take off their paddings, helmets, and uniforms, that is when injury reveals itself. We'll call them Football Player A.

At other times, football players—we'll call them Football Player B—experience abrupt pain, which can bring a player to their knees in the middle of the game with thousands of fans looking at them. I believe this is the truth for a number of people. Some people are waking up every day, going to work, caring for others, attending events with a smile on their face, but secretly hurting. Other people experience adverse pain that causes them to isolate, stay in bed, mistreat others, or lash out. People are doing life with a broken heart, a bruised foot, and a pounding headache. The worst part is, they are ignoring it. They do not acknowledge the impact it is having on their lives. I would boldly say that people are operating mindlessly and tragically missing the abundant life they are born into.

I used to be one of these people. I didn't know that I was living while hurting. I didn't know that my heart was broken from past relationships, I just kept on living. I did not realize that I was moving slowly in life because my foot was bruised. I ignored the pounding headaches. My mindset was limited and toxic, and my self-esteem was low. All my pain was keeping me from fully enjoying life. Life's still moments, which we can think of as the locker room, revealed my truth after a while. It will reveal yours too.

I attended a four-year college right after high school. Towards the end of my senior year of college, I started dating a guy, who is now my husband. He is the opposite of me. I am meek and he is outgoing. I am cautious and he is a risk taker. I committed myself to him early in our relationship, and we decided to date with the intention of getting married. You see, my broken heart, bruised foot, and headache manifested like a dragon being released from its cage for the first time in a thousand years. Behind the mask of dating a law student, living downtown on Washington Ave., attending graduate school, and looking fly. Yet, I was suffering, but

I kept on living. I was like Football Player A. I did not know I was hurting, and I just kept playing in the game.

Have you ever felt ready to heal from trauma, depression, or anxiety? Have you ever said to yourself *"This can't be it?"* Are you tired of wearing a mask, acting like you are okay when you are not? Do you feel stuck, and no amount of caffeine can make that feeling go away? Have you ever been in my shoes? Do you ever feel like God is trying to deliver you, but something is blocking that deliverance? If you said yes to any of these questions, this book was written for you. This book is intended for people who believe in Jesus Christ and are secretly struggling with low self-esteem, identity issues, trauma, and relationship issues. I encourage you to read this book with others to get to the root of your emotions.

Throughout this book, I will share stories and use analogies to explain various concepts to help you heal from the inside out. I will help you get to the root of your behaviors, patterns, and emotions. Take this journey with me and use my stories to help identify your truth. This book is not here to say if you are right, healthy, or have a mental health disorder. Rather, this book should be used as a tool to support.

I am a huge fan of journaling your thoughts and emotions. At the end of each chapter, you will get a much-needed time to reflect on yourself and life experiences in the Root Check-ins. So, get ready to reflect and heal. Do yourself a favor, take time to reflect and process your feelings as you read each chapter. You will have exercises to complete that will direct you to get to the root in different areas of your life. Getting to the root means identifying the root cause for X, Y, and Z.

Choose to get to down to the core of your triggers and mood swings. Peel back layers to gain clarity about your habits and thought processes. It will help you understand yourself more. If you understand yourself better, you will learn how to manage and cope. Knowledge breeds power. You have power to accept, change, or tolerate things. Each Root Check-ins will empower you to learn coping concepts and strategies. These are actual exercises that I use with my clients and in my personal life gain clarity about their mood and heart.

My ultimate desire is for you to join my Virtual Healing Circles (VHC) to encourage people to seek God for a renewed mind. A VHC inspires people to get to the root of their pain to unveil the abundant life that they are destined for. I hope that at the conclusion of this book, you will feel empowered to surrender your heart to God. I pray that you will only hunger for the bread of life and thirst from the living water. I pray that you will know the truth about yourself, and you will never ever doubt yourself again.

P.S. Hey… One last point: Healing can occur instantly like warming up food in the microwave, or it can occur over time like cooking food in a crockpot. Either way, you are heading in the right direction.

P.S.S. Some topics and stories may be triggering for you. I discuss suicide, depression, and anxiety. If you find yourself triggered, please take a break and care for yourself using healthy coping skills.

Chapter 1
The Acknowledgment Root

"A wound that goes unacknowledged and unwept is a wound that cannot heal." – John Eldrege

Picture it: Illinois in 2018. Before COVID-19 and in a mask-free world. I was sitting in a booth with two friends at Panera Bread one Saturday morning. The café was buzzing with chatter, fingers clicking the keys on laptops, and the bagel slicer cutting bagels in half. I had just scarfed down my breakfast sandwich, and now I was sipping on lemon water. My friends were talking about their jobs, kids, and relationships. I was listening. Typically, in group of three or more people, I am the listener. I listen and observe people's body language. I try to pick up on non-verbal cues to see how a person feels, only adding my two cents to the conversation when necessary. Today, my friends noticed that I was quieter than normal. They turned and asked if I was okay. Suddenly, tears rolled down my cheeks. I pulled the hood over my head and pulled the strings. I hide my face in my hoodie.

I did not want anyone to see me crying in public. For goodness' sake, I was in Panera Bread on a Saturday. Anyone was bound to walk in and see me. My friends were awesome. They consoled me and asked what was going on. You see, on the outside, I am a dime piece. The total package. A part of a power couple. The woman

1

who has it all together. It was true, on paper. I am the CEO of a private counseling practice, the wife of a lawyer, a mother of two vibrant children, owner of a $277k house, a member of the most elite sorority, and not to mention a servant of Jesus. My life was a fairy tale. It was picture perfect. On the outside looking in, I appeared happy and blessed by the Best. Yet I was in a booth in a crowded café crying because I did not feel fulfilled.

I had been battling depression, anxiety, and insecurities for a long time. I believe the depression and anxiety started after having kids. I experienced postpartum depression after the first pregnancy. I had struggled with insecurities since I was a child. I always felt like I was not enough. I sought for validation and acceptance. I thought I did not fit in anywhere. I would hide my true feelings by being overly committed to things, trying to make my name great, and getting excessively involved in our children's lives. I was a stressed-out helicopter mom.

As I cried in the café shielding my face from the possible judgment of strangers, my friends advised me to seek counseling. I was shocked and embarrassed. I am a therapist. I counsel children, teens, and adults. I help others. Did I really need counseling? Had it gotten that bad that I, the counselor, needed to be counseled? My friend said, "You need to call HER."

I know you are like, "Who is HER?" No, I am not talking about the pop singer H.E.R. I am talking about an emotional midwife, also known as a spiritual counselor. I called and told her that I was ready to heal.

You see, I was living life as Football Player A. I mentioned in the introduction that football players are notorious for playing the game even while they are in pain. Some players ignore it, and others realize it only after the game when they are resting in the locker room. I was the player who was playing all four quarters continuously and ignoring my pain. My silent pain became so apparent that I was not able to keep tears from falling on my cheeks at a coffee shop. That silent pain was no longer quiet.

I was relieved that I had finally said something to someone. It was like I was holding my breath for a long time and could finally breathe again. I thought if I said how I really felt, that my husband, friends, or heck the world would think that I am not fit to be a chief executive officer of a newly launched counseling practice in Illinois. By telling my friends how I really felt, I realized I was not crazy or an incompetent counselor. I understood that everyone at some part of their lives will: A) acknowledge how they are feeling, B) confront their past, childhood, and/or traumatic events, and C) choose to be healed.

When I was sitting in the coffee shop with my hoodie over my head and tears rolling down my cheeks, I decided that I wanted to be healed. I strongly desired to feel whole and like a woman. I desired to be mentally strong and secure. I wanted to trust people and not look at others suspiciously. I wanted a new mindset about myself and my future. I wanted better relationships with my husband, kids, and family. I no longer wanted to be surface with people, nor did I want to keep wearing the "Fake it till you make it" mask. I was so over feeling little, small, limited, and invisible. I knew God placed me here for a reason. The way I felt was not adding up to the abundant life I was reading about in the Bible.

Can you relate to me? I know I am not the only person who had a "coming to Jesus" moment. It is in that very moment you feel so low that the only way up is to go to Jesus and face the facts. Literally, when I came home from lunch with my friends, I went to my prayer room, and I got on my knees and asked Jesus to help me. I felt like I could not keep living life silently suffering while seeming well off in public. I was lying to myself, clients, family, and church. I was literally living a double life. I truly believe God heard me, because things started to shift.

A few weeks after I had my "coming to Jesus" moment, I attended an event. Let me tell you what happened. It was as if God himself confirmed that I needed to get to the root to heal.

I branded myself as the Empowerment Coach and Counselor with the help of a business coach. My coach was awesome and well established. I admired her so much, and I wanted my business to grow like hers. She was comfortable in her skin, and she had a lot of connections. She was assertive, determined, and poised. She possessed qualities that I was aiming for. My coach helped me establish my business goals and an executive plan to fulfill the desired outcome. She hosted annual workshops, and this particular year, she asked me along with several other participants in her services to be guest panelists. I was enthralled. As a guest panelist, I was directed to share how the business coach's services had improved my business and life.

During that time, all I was focused on was making my name great. I was a new entrepreneur, and I was thirsty for clients. I wanted people to like me, know me, and book me for speaking engagements. I planned to use the opportunity to generate new business.

I looked super cute that day. I wore a black blazer, my custom-designed business t-shirt, blue jeans, and black booties. My hair and make-up were on point. I had hair extensions, so my hair was long, wavy, and full. I was a little nervous because I did not know what I was going to say. I was going to wing it. I attended the event with one of my friends who has always supported me in different adventures. When we walked in, I was overwhelmed by the number of participants and the amount of beauty in the room. There were so many professional women in the gathering. All I could think was, "I want this. I want to know and relate to so many women. I want to host an event like this, but little old me doesn't know that many people." I was lusting. (Side note: Lusting is not always sexual. It just means to greatly desire, covet, or long after something.) I was daydreaming of hosting my own workshop. Some women entrepreneurs were vendors who sold their products, and others were guests. The room was full of fierce, educated women.

My thoughts immediately started going haywire. I started questioning my value, wondering if I should have dressed differently, and thinking, "What am I going to say?" I felt like a little girl in a room with grown women. What was I doing there? I went to the restroom just to be alone for a few seconds. I forced myself to use the restroom, and then I looked in the mirror and had an out-of-body experience. I was shocked when I saw my reflection. I truly felt like a small, little girl getting ready to speak to well-established, secure women, yet standing in the mirror was a beautiful, established woman. I looked like I belonged in the room and as a panelist, even though I felt like a scared, insecure girl. I shook my head, fluffed out my hair, and ignored that feeling.

But soon, that same feeling happened again. It was time for the guest panelists to sit at the head of the room. We stood and took pictures, and then the host introduced each panelist. I was last to speak, and I just knew I had to bring. I had to sell myself, make people believe in my slogan so they would hire me for future events. I was telling myself, "Bring it home, girl, you got this. Convince them." When it was my time to speak, I felt like I was a little girl telling a huge lie. I was very insecure, standing there judging and criticizing myself as

I was talking. Do not get me wrong, God has truly blessed me with a gift to counsel others and empower them to work through their emotions – I just haven't processed mine.

I could no longer "fake it till I make it." I wanted to be real and authentic. I had to get to the root of why I felt like a little girl even as a thirty-three-year-old adult. I started assessing the source. I started looking at the root of my issues.

THE ROOT CHECK-IN #1

Hey, I know you are like, "Whoa, I am not the only one who has crying spells and does not wholly understand what is wrong with me." Rest assured, you are not alone in any of your feelings. In fact, you will discover that so many people experience similar struggles. This is why I think the human race is so unique. We are different, yet so alike.

This is your first Root Check-in. I want you to take time to simply process your feelings. Give yourself this time to acknowledge your thoughts and feelings. How does your body feel right now? Are you relaxed or tense? _____

_____

_____

_____

_____

I have been feeling lately.... _____

_____

_____

_____

_____

Because... _____

_____

_____

_____

_____

Get to the Root!

I want.... _____

_____

_____

_____

_____

I am reading this guide because... _____

_____

_____

_____

_____

_____

_____

Chapter 2
The Childhood Root

———— • ● ● ● • ————

"All of us are products of our childhood."
— Michael Jackson

WARNING: some parts of the content may be triggering for readers. I encourage you to pause, address your feelings, use coping skills, and/or talk to a trusted person. Resume reading the book when you are ready.

According to Charles Whitfield, a psychotherapist and author of *The Child Within*[1], adults have a child within. I beckon for this to be true. I really felt like a little girl living an adult life. Whitfield states that the child within is your true self or authentic self. This notion was confirmed when I saw my counselor. My first session was mind-blowing. I was truly looking forward to unpacking why I had been crying, why I felt insecure despite being successful on the outside. I also wanted to acknowledge why I felt like a little girl and strongly wanted to feel grown. I went to counseling on Valentine's Day in 2019. I arrived at her office early. I was a little nervous because I did not know what to expect as the recipient of emotional support, as I have always been the counselor. I thought the session was going to be for one hour. No, it was not. It was three hours of me unpacking my life. This session was ordained by God.

My emotional midwife prompted me to describe my family dynamic during my childhood. I lived with my immediate family, and occasionally some other family members lived with us. I was the youngest of four children. My mother worked full time, and sometimes overnight, while my father had various jobs.

Parents are the first relationship a kid has. It is the first example of how to build communication skills, trust, and love. The parent demonstrates appropriate expectations and boundaries. The opposite is true too: An unhealthy attachment with parents can lead a child to dysfunctional communication skills, insecurity, and fears. According to Dr. Diane Benoit (2004), "The quality of attachment that an infant develops with a specific caregiver is largely determined by the caregiver's response to the infant when the infant's attachment system is 'activated.'" She goes on to say that "the quality of the infant-parent attachment is a powerful predictor of a child's later social and emotional outcome."[2]

I have keen memories with my mom and dad from when I was growing up. However, I felt distant from my family. I was reserved and passive. I shared my feelings with my mother by letter – I used to write her expressing how I felt. I wanted to have a close relationship with my father. I experienced a few traumatic incidents during my childhood that left me quiet, as if I did not have a voice. I was reserved. I was meek. I enjoyed being alone, and I stayed in my room often. My siblings made jokes about me. I was a loner.

I liked being by myself, but I really wanted a lot of friends like my older sister. Growing up, she was always on the phone talking to a friend. People called her all the time. Me, on the other hand, I had one or two friends to call me. I did have friends, but even then, I maintained relationships on a surface level. I was insecure about myself. I struggled with feeling worthy and important. My mom would tell me how special I was and encourage me. She even told me that I had invisible angel's wings on my back. I did not believe it. I wanted to believe her and not wear masks in front of people. I always wanted to please my parents and others. I did not want to ruffle any feathers. I had many thoughts and feelings; I just did not express them. I did not know if anyone would listen. Everyone was living – they were like Football Player A. I did not think my thoughts mattered.

I held my thoughts within so tight for so long that I had thoughts of wanting to die. I was less than 13 years old when I had that thought. I was sitting in my bedroom at my vanity set, looking at myself in the mirror crying and thinking I was ugly. I had all these tormenting thoughts flowing through my head. I was so tired of thinking something was wrong with me. "Why am I reserved? Why don't I like myself? Why is this my life?" I suffered in silence, and so do others. When I hear clients say they have thoughts of wanting to die, I have sympathy and my ears are tuned in. I understand. Sometimes people want the pain to stop. People are looking for relief, and they think that is the way. According to Healthwise, "Most people who seriously consider suicide do not want to die. Rather, they see suicide as a solution to a problem and a way to end their pain. People who seriously consider suicide feel hopeless, helpless, and worthless. A person who feels hopeless believes that no one can help with a particular event or problem."[3]

Thinking about ending your life by suicide is not the resolution people truly seek. Death is tragic and permanent. It ends your pain on earth, but other people's pain of grief begins. It is best to contact a professional counselor to help sort through your emotions, feelings, and current situation. My mother sent me to a counselor for emotional support. I wasn't ready, and I showed up with a stank attitude. Every question the therapist asked, I gave her one word. What I really wanted was to learn how to talk with my mom. I wanted to tell her how I really felt, and I wanted to feel better about myself. But I kept living like Football Player A.

Various psychotherapists suggest peeling back the layers of your childhood to understand who you are. I recommend that you take a look at your interactions with your parents and caregivers, because childhood shapes your mind, perception, and behaviors. Looking back, I did not have accurate perceptions of myself. I thought I was lame for not having a lot of friends like my sister. I thought I was not likable, so I choose not to foster meaningful relationships. I was afraid of being rejected, when I was never actually rejected by people, I just assumed that I did not have anything to offer. It's so interesting to look back with hindsight and realize how having an inaccurate perception impacts adulthood. A person's perception, how they perceive a situation, becomes their reality.

In my case, my perception was this: "I am small. I do not have a lot of friends, so I am lame. I am a loner, therefore something is wrong with me. I am afraid to hang out with people because they may not like me. I do not have much to say. I witnessed and was involved in a few scary situations. We do not talk about things after they happen. I do not like myself. Something is wrong with me." My limiting perceptions became my beliefs and reality.

THINKING BACK, WHAT WAS YOUR CHILDHOOD LIKE? HOW DID YOU PERCEIVE YOURSELF AND YOUR ENVIRONMENT?

Children are dependent on their parents and caregivers to cultivate a healthy mentality and outlook about their future. Parents and caregivers are models and the prominent voice in their children's lives. There are two voices that shape a child's self-esteem: their environment and their parents. Sometimes the voices are competing, and sometimes they are in harmony. I believe that children are born with a clean mental slate. The do not have a high or low self-perception. They do not know if they are worthy or not. They are unaware of being accepted versus rejected until they interact with their parents or caregivers. After a baby has lived for a few weeks, they begin to understand the power of connection. After a child is born, doctors recommend that the baby lays on their mother's uncovered chest. This is called "Skin to Skin," and it helps foster a bond. They realize they are not alone in this big world. They are the most dependent creature, besides the elderly. They are taught how to trust, how to be affectionate, depending on whether they are accepted or rejected based on the actions and behaviors of their primary caregiver.

With children, nothing has influenced their self-perception but genes, events, and parents. I have two children, and I remember how they would react every time I clapped after they put their shoes on the correct feet. They were so proud of themselves and smiled with confidence. I can also recall how they look when I yell at them. My son says, "You are being mean to me." Those examples shape my children's minds and perceptions. They like praise, but they do not like being yelled at.

WHAT ARE SOME MEMORIES YOU RECALL THAT SHAPED YOUR VIEW ABOUT YOURSELF AND THE WORLD?

I have counseled hundreds of adults who present with relationship issues and have low self-esteem. I want you to know, based on research and my years of experience in counseling, these struggles can start in your primary years and after major life experiences.

Both quality and deficient social skills transfer into adulthood. For example, I was afraid to tell my mom how I really felt as a kid, and then I struggled with speaking up about concerns within marriage as an adult. Another example is that I was afraid of being rejected by my peers because some of them made jokes about me in junior high school. Well, as an adult, I had the tendency to keep relationships surface-level to avoid being rejected again. The same is true if a child grows up with a parent who abuses drugs or struggles with mental health issues; it impacts how a child thinks interactions are supposed to go. On some occasions, adults can find the root of their behaviors in events that occurred during childhood.

I believe in the power of Jesus Christ. I believe the word of God and incorporate it in sessions with clients who are also believers. I respect people, beliefs, and cultures. I believe it is so amazing how big and diverse our world is. Yet, when I have a client who believes in Christ, the sessions tend to go differently. We can discuss their relationship with Christ and how it relates to their perceptions.

In the next chapter, we will learn how to start assessing how your childhood and life events impact your self-perception and life.

THE ROOT CHECK-IN #2

How was your relationship with your parent(s) or caregiver(s) during your childhood? Rate the quality of your relationship. Circle 1-10. (1 represents low/poor and 10 represents high/great.)

[__|__|__|__|__|__|__|__|__|__]
1. 2. 3. 4. 5. 6. 7. 8. 9. 10

What could have made the relationship better? _____

_____

_____

_____

What did you need from your parents/caregivers? _____

_____

_____

_____

What was your perception of yourself during childhood? Did you struggle with depression or anxiety as a child? _____

_____

_____

_____

Chapter 3
The Self-Discovery Root

"The best way to heal is in three relationships, with true self, with safe others and with God." – Charles Whitfield

Now that our eyes have been enlightened by the fact that some of our emotional and social issues stem from childhood and other life experiences, let's explore how it manifests in our lives. I typically receive phone calls from potential clients because their emotions are on level 10, and it is interfering with their work and relationships. People start realizing the effects that unresolved depression, anxiety, and trauma can cause on their daily lives. Sometimes, major life changes can impact your life negatively. For instance, fostering a child, giving birth to a child, a new job, COVID, or changes in your schedule can impact your mood and daily life.

Understand that mental health issues or stress can hit you like a ton of bricks, or slowly like your eyes opening from a night of rest. It is like Football Player A has finally made it to the locker room, and they are removing all their gear. The pain from getting tackled during the game of life is becoming prevalent. I can relate to my clients and to Football Player A. I was silently hit after having our first child. You see, as a counselor, I knew all the signs of depression and anxiety. I knew that if a person is suffering from depression, they are likely to experience:

- Depressed mood most of the day, nearly every day.

- Markedly diminished interest or pleasure in all, or almost all, activities most of the day, nearly every day.

- Significant weight loss when not dieting or weight gain or decrease or increase in appetite nearly every day.

- A slowing down of thought and a reduction of physical movement (observable by others, not merely subjective feelings of restlessness or being slowed down).

- Fatigue or loss of energy nearly every day.

- Feelings of worthlessness or excessive or inappropriate guilt nearly every day.

- Diminished ability to think or concentrate, or indecisiveness, nearly every day.

- Recurrent thoughts of death, recurrent suicidal ideation without a specific plan, or a suicide attempt or a specific plan for committing suicide.[4]

When I was pregnant with our first child, I told myself, "I will not get postpartum depression." I told myself, "I will remain the same after I have my child." When I went to parenting classes, they reminded me of all the signs of postpartum depression, but I was so prideful that I dismissed their warnings. I told myself, "I got this." Boy oh boy, I was in total denial. I was depressed and I did not even know it. When I went to the doctor for my follow-up appointments, I disregarded the depression quiz, answering "not likely" on all the questions.

I realized I was not okay one day when my husband and I were sitting on the coach watching television with our daughter, who was playing around us. Our living room had toys everywhere, and we had just finished eating pizza. At the time, I was an at-home mother. So, I was with the baby all day by myself because all my friends worked during the day. As we were sitting on the couch, I remember feeling annoyed and uncomfortable. I was like a pot of boiling water. I was bubbling. Our daughter was laughing and enjoying life. She crawled up on the right side of my arm, and I screamed at her, "GET OFF OF ME!" I was upset and annoyed. My husband looked at me as if I were crazy. I rolled my shoulders back, stood up abruptly, and stormed to our bedroom and locked the door.

Don't get me wrong, one blow-up is not a sign of depression or postpartum depression. It is a series of similar events that indicated that I was not emotionally stable. I was dealing with major life changes all at once, and I pridefully ignored the telltale signs of my mood. Before I was an at-home mom, I lived in St. Louis in a popular community, I worked full time, saw my friends regularly, and had a lot of freedom. Then suddenly, I moved back to Illinois, my friends and spouse worked full-time, and I became an at-home caregiver. I was torn, debating whether I should stay home to care for our new baby or go back to work full-time. I wanted a professional name for myself. I wanted to elevate in my career, and I needed social worker hours to obtain licensures. I was feeling like all my peers were advancing and I was at home folding clothes, cooking, and cleaning. I felt low about myself. I did not have co-workers to eat lunch with or chat with, and I was alone most of the time with a baby. My husband had just passed the bar exam, and he was adjusting to his first job as a city prosecutor. My life had become totally different.

I had several incidents like the one mentioned above. I also had a low mood, and I did not take care of myself. I remember my first Mother's Day. I was super tired, but I was excited to celebrate that day with my baby girl. At my church, they took pictures of mothers with their children. I remember the picture captured how I felt – as they say, a picture is worth a thousand words. Before I had a child, I wore heels, I kept my hair styled, and I dressed cute. I was no diva, but I always looked together. In my first Mother's Day picture, I looked beat down and unkempt. My daughter looked adorable, but I did not look well at all. I was emotionally upset and grateful at the same time. When I look back at that picture, I knew I was not in a good place. I had lost interest in keeping up with my appearance. I devoted so much of my attention and energy to my growing family that I dismissed my own needs.

Another time, my husband and I had friends over our house. Our friends were another married couple who had a toddler who played well with our daughter. My husband and our friends were sitting in the living room talking about random issues and watching the girls build a tower with blocks. I came out of our bedroom and sat on the floor next to the girls. I looked up at my husband and dear friends, and I abruptly said, "I am depressed." The room went silent. It was like Football Player B suddenly fell in the middle of the field due to pulling his hamstring. Man down. A flag on the play. Guess what happened next. No one said anything. The room went silent.

I was vulnerable. I spoke my truth, but I retracted my statement when everyone was quiet. I felt small and lonely. My husband, the man I lay next to every night, did not even know how I was feeling. I guess I never had the words to describe that I felt down and I didn't know how to handle parenting, my personal life, and my desire to return to work. I was not feeling like myself, and I wanted to feel like a woman. Before I had a child, I felt like I had everything in order and my house was neat. After having a child, I felt like nothing was in order, I would forget things often, and somewhere, after stepping into this new role, I lost my mojo.

After my second birth, I was mentally tormented by this ruminating thought of "All of this does not matter." I had the constant thought that all my efforts in being a good mother and sexy wife would not matter because it all fades away. Those thoughts were sucking life out of me. When I was up in the middle of the night breastfeeding our son, I would think, "You are doing all of this for nothing." When I was intentionally exposing our daughter to new environments, I had these underlining thoughts of "It does not matter." I was kind of living in fear. I was experiencing spiritual warfare. No one knew I had those thoughts. I suffered quietly, and it impacted my life drastically. I was trying to fight through it by showing up for my family each day, but man was it tough.

Have you ever had inner battles, and it seemed like you couldn't tell anyone because you thought they would not understand? I have been there. I believe that some people have outer battles, like relationships or job struggles, but my battles were silent and inner. No one could really tell how much I was suffering because I know how to show up.

DO YOU HAVE INNER OR OUTER BATTLES?

In that moment, I realized that people do not openly admit that things are wrong. No one was really talking about their feelings. No one really said if they were stressed out. All I saw was people self-medicating or masking. People did not know how to cope, and I realized I did not how to cope either. Individuals appeared to be walking around stressed, overeating, smoking marijuana, drinking during the day, and self-indulging to manage the stress of being an adult.

In that moment, my husband and friends were shocked. They did not have an immediate response, but eventually, they asked me questions. Nothing really changed after I openly admitted that I was dealing with postpartum depression. I just kept living. I felt sad, insecure, and tired of doing life, but I kept on parenting and being a wife. I kept showing up despite how I felt on the inside.

> **KUDOS FOR ALL THE PEOPLE WHO KEEP SHOWING UP TO DO LIFE EVEN THOUGH YOU MIGHT NOT FEEL GREAT ALL OF THE TIME.**

Let's be honest, adulting is not easy. I was trying to adult from a depressed and broken state. I was trying to cultivate a family from a place of insecurity, and I was failing. I was trying to connect with my husband broken. I was relating and fostering friendships from a place of pain and fear of rejection. I was raising our children from a place of passivity. My unstable mood and unhealed hurt were impacting every area of my life.

The power of self-reflection is the key to exposing those unwanted emotions and behaviors. Reflecting or turning the mirror to observe how you really feel will give you great insight. Ignoring your emotions are no longer acceptable. Emotions are not bad. Emotions paints a picture of your thoughts, wants, and need. They are internal signals. Society has given the following emotions a negative connation; anger, fear, sadness, and loneliness. Those feelings are signs of a deeper need or want. For examples, fear can express your need for safety or comfort. Sadness may say you have a need for support or happiness. Loneliness may show a desire for social interaction or companionship. Anger may express need for clarity, understanding or resolution.

Emotions are not our enemy. Emotions are our friends. They warn us, validates our thoughts, and express how we are really feeling. As a woman and as a clinician, I understand that no one likes to be a constant state of sadness, anger or anxiety. As you continue reading the book, you will learn how to manage your emotions. But first, take time to identify your emotions. If you need help connecting feelings to its name, go to https://www.therapistaid. com/worksheets/emotions-language-signs-behaviors.pdf to view the Emotion Reference Sheet. It is a great resource to help you gain clarity between your thoughts, signs and related behaviors.

THE ROOT CHECK-IN #3

Acknowledge your raw and unfiltered thoughts about your life...

_____

_____

_____

_____

_____

_____

Understanding yourself is one of many keys to getting to the root. You have so many feelings and behaviors. You are allowed to feel. You are also responsible for managing your emotions. Naming your emotions and behaviors empowers you to recall wanted and unwanted feelings in the future.

**Special note, you are entitled to your emotions, but be aware of them so you do not harm yourself or others.

Root Reflection: _____

_____

_____

_____

_____

_____

_____

_____

Chapter 4
Get to the Root Part 1

———— • • ● • • ————

"The steps of insecurity: Comparison, Compensation,
Competition, Compulsion, Condemnation, Control."
— unknown

Have you ever seen an older kid trying to boss around a younger kid? The older kid thinks they know everything, and the younger kid talks back to the older kid, and then they start arguing. That is exactly how I was parenting my kids during their toddler years. It was a hot mess. Parenting is not for the faint of heart. It is resourceful to have your spiritual, physical, financial, and emotional capacity intact. I am going to try to explain how each area showed my shortcomings and how spiritual and mental healing freed me from the cycle of frustration.

I was emotionally immature and sought constant validation from my kids. I was parenting from a little girl's perspective and as an overly zealous parent. I was excessively concerned about my kids' future. Let me be honest, I was fearful of their future. From the little girl's perspective, I found myself getting easily frustrated when they did not act or do what I wanted. My mood would go from zero to 100 in .5 seconds. I wanted to control them. I had to tell myself repeatedly that my kids are not robots to help myself deescalate.

I began to realize that something was wrong with my emotions and perspective when I kept asking my mom, "What is wrong with me? Why do I feel so bad after I discipline my daughter?" Often, I found myself feeling guilty for taking something away from her or yelling at her due to her misbehavior. Our biggest conflicts started in the mornings before school. It seems like every morning we had a disagreement, and I felt bad for hours after dropping her off at school. In my mind, I told myself that I was a bad parent, my daughter was going to be damaged, and she would internalize my poor skills and it would negatively impact her as an adult. I literally thought that when I had a disagreement or had to be a firm parent, I was failing. I thought that I was a failure because my kids did not listen to me.

I literally tried to be a perfect mother. However, I was actually sabotaging myself and felt like I was in a constant state of defeat. For instance, my daughter would pick out her clothes for school. In the winter months, I wanted her to wear an undershirt, and if she came downstairs without one, I would send her back to her room to get one. Then she would complain, and I internalize it. This was the ugly cycle: I give her an instruction, she talks back, I get frustrated, I start to have negative self-talk, she stomps away, and then I think that I am a bad parent.

My core beliefs were:

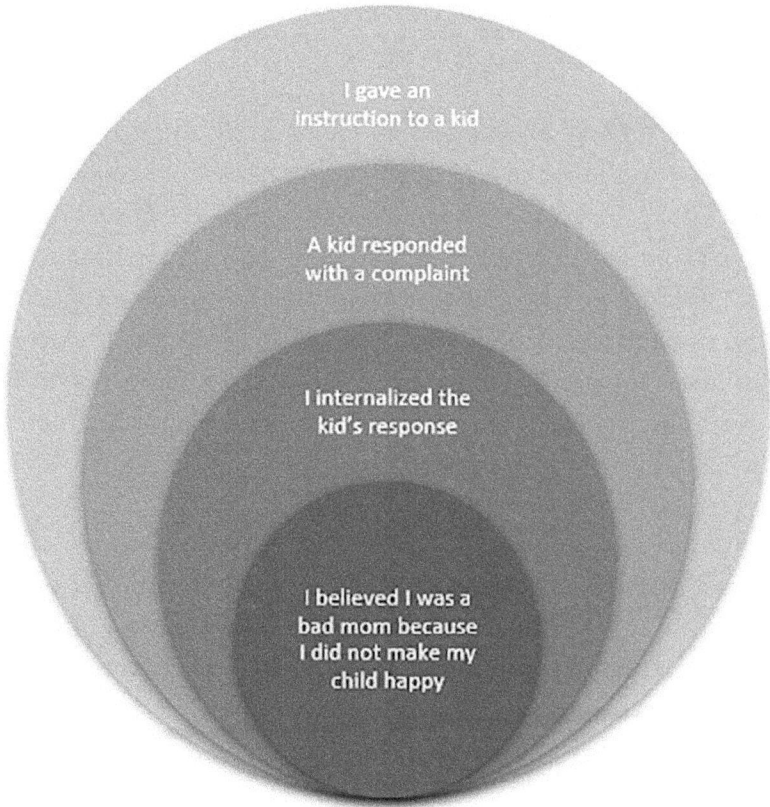

I gave an
instruction to a kid

A kid responded
with a complaint

I internalized the
kid's response

I believed I was a
bad mom because
I did not make my
child happy

This ugly core belief caused me to feel angry, insecure, and annoyed. That negative pattern of thoughts and actions taught my daughter that she could push my buttons. I found myself praying for God to show me where I was failing. "Why is parenting so hard? Why don't my kids do what I expect?" I talked to God about my social work credentials and how I taught parenting classes for months at a mental health agency. I was wondering why all this knowledge was not being transferred to real life. I cried and prayed.

Just like when I felt depressed, I talked to my husband, older women, my friends, and even a therapist. They listened to me vent how frustrated I felt. They offered strategies and support. I was heard, but nothing changed at home.

I started observing my triggers and how I felt afterward. I noticed that I gave my kids several chances without consequences, they ignored me and kept doing what was fun in the moment, and I felt social pressures to be a certain kind of mother because I am Black. Black mothers are known for being hard, stern, and not taking mess from kids. I struggled with being hard, stern, and emotionless towards my kids. I realized that my defeating thoughts were the hindrance. God revealed that I was enmeshed with and co-dependent on my daughter.

According to David Prior, LMFT, "Enmeshment is a description of a relationship between two people in which personal boundaries are permeable and unclear."[5] It could also mean that one person takes on the emotions of another person. I was enmeshed with my daughter. When I made a decision or gave her a consequence, she was upset (as she should have been), and I would feel bad or low. I would doubt myself by questioning if I was parenting right. I took on my daughter's emotions. If my daughter was happy, I felt happy, and vice versa. Enmeshment can occur within romantic relationships and families. I started to notice that I was enmeshed with my sister and husband as well. My mood would alter based on their emotions towards me.

I also realized that I was addicted to making people happy because my emotions were entangled with others. That entangled web of trying to make people happy because my happiness depended on their level of contentment is emotionally draining. I was a people pleaser and a co-dependent parent. I feared my children rejecting me when I disciplined them. I wanted to be a cool, friendly, approachable parent. I was looking for acceptance from our kids. Listen, when I understood that I was trying to make my kids happy to validate myself as a parent, I knew that I had to get to the root of this painful truth.

Have you noticed that you are trying to get people to accept you? Are you trying to please people to be accepted? Are you a parent who has enmeshed your feelings or worth based on the responses from your kids? Do you do things just to make people happy with you? I did not know I was living that way. I did not realize my dependency on my kids. I was only aware of how emotionally distraught I felt at the start and end of the day.

One way to start releasing yourself from people pleasing and co-dependency is to become aware of your mood. It is important to know your baseline mood, which is how you feel when you are not stressed, bothered, tired, or hungry. I am typically calm, in a good mood, content, peaceful, grateful, and aware. Anything I feel outside of my baseline, I closely monitor.

WHAT IS YOUR BASELINE? DESCRIBE HOW YOU FEEL WHEN YOU ARE NOT STRESSED, BOTHERED, OR HUNGRY.

I noticed that I was angry doing nice things for my kids. That seems a little odd, but deep down, that was how I felt. For instance, this might seem so minuscule, but it gave me insight on how my mood fluctuates. I told my kids that I would take them to get a treat. The whole day, we were out and about. When it was time to go home, my daughter reminded me that I told them I would take them to get a treat. Mind you, it was 10pm. I was tired and ready to go to bed. I unwillingly took them to the store. I was rushing them, and

I lowkey had a bad attitude. I gave them 30 seconds to pick out a treat. They got candy at 10pm, so then I became worried about their bodies, teeth, and dreams (you know sugar can interfere with your dreams.) Now, most of you would say, "You should keep your word." I will not argue with you about that; however, instead of exercising my positive authority by telling them that they would get a treat the next day due to it being late at night, I voided my thoughts to avoid my daughter having an attitude because she did not get her way.

At the end of the day, I was more concerned about my daughter's mood than my own. My mood was irritable because I did something that I did not think was best. It is important that we honor our word to teach our kids about having a noble character, but it is also okay for parents to follow through on their word another day. I needed to honor myself and separate myself from my daughter's emotions. In hindsight, I realize I do that often. I put their wants before my needs. In return, I secretly have meltdowns by complaining to others about how my kids do not respect me and they act entitled. Ummm, REALITY CHECK. I contributed to our dynamic. I did not have boundaries. A house without boundaries is vulnerable. In retrospect, were my kids doing anything wrong? No, they were only doing what I allowed them to do.

To overcome enmeshment, I had to know my identity as a parent. I am here to disciple them. God has called me to direct our children onto the right path, and when they are older, they will not leave it (Proverbs 22:6). I am to teach our kids to follow through on their commitments and model a noble character. However, I am not called to be used, manipulated, or ignored. I had to stop blaming my kids for my feelings. I am responsible for my own reactions. I had to mature and assess who was parenting. I had to differentiate between the little girl inside of me who longed to be accepted from my adult self who wanted to connect and train our kids in the right way to go.

In my efforts to seek God about my co-dependency and enmeshment, I recalled the words of a pastor who said, "In order to get something different, I have to do something differently." I wanted to have a different interaction with my kids. I prostrated on the ground in prayer. The Lord spoke to me and said, "I love you. You are good. I made every part of you. I want you. You are special. The fear of rejection is a tactic. Every part of you I made. Your mother birthed you, but I created you. I stitched you. I molded you and formed you. I have given you a godly identity, not a world identity. Not a title-based identity in your kids, husband, and career. Those things did not create or give you an identity. I gave it to you when I formed you in your mother's womb before time started. Your identity was there. You are good. You are complete, not incomplete. I saw all that I made, and it was very good." After listening to God's heart about me, I wrote it down. I meditated on it and declared it over my life. My heart believed his words, and I gradually started coaching myself away from depending on my family and roles. I learned that I needed to separate my emotions from my kids.

Both my mother and a counselor told me to stop taking my kids' behavior so personally. They told me that kids see how far they can go with their parents. Kids intentionally try their parents, push the limits, and test their parents' patience. Though I carried our children for nine months, breastfed them for six months, and worked hard to ensure we would have a flexible income, they are their own people. They are individuals. The umbilical cord was cut at the time of delivery. We each have our own set of thoughts, emotions, and responses. I am responsible for their spiritual growth, education, and basic needs, but I am not responsible for their emotions.

As I walk in this light of individuality, I am more emotionally stable. Now, when I tell my daughter to put on an undershirt because it is cold outside, she still becomes grumpy and tries to reason with me. I do a quick body scan to check my mood, disposition, and hunger level. I take a step back, look for the true problem, and explain the course of action. When my daughter gets upset, I acknowledge how she feels, but I restate the rule. I also give her space to feel by saying, "You can feel angry, or you can disagree, but I will not tolerate disrespect." I also tell myself, "Those are her feelings. My emotions are not swayed to the left or right."

I am learning to home in on my rules, godly identity, and honoring myself. I am still compassionate towards my kids. I explained to my daughter our individuality and how she should not be ruled by another person's emotions or remarks. I still coach myself to stay within my bubble of emotions, thoughts, and responses as I radically accept their bubbles.

THE ROOT CHECK-IN #4

Take a deep breath. Inhale and exhale.

Processing your relationships and recognizing how you feel in them is not easy. Admitting how your core beliefs are impacting your life takes guts. As you get to the root of your behaviors, remember to be patient and gentle with yourself. Personal improvement can make you emotional or cause you to think poorly about yourself. You might wonder, "Why did I do this or that?" or "Why would I allow myself to...." No judgment here. This is your safe place. Observe and reflect without judgment.

This section was meant to illustrate how your core beliefs will impact you daily and in relationships. Your core beliefs may be negative and/or positive. Regardless of the category, confess your core beliefs about yourself.

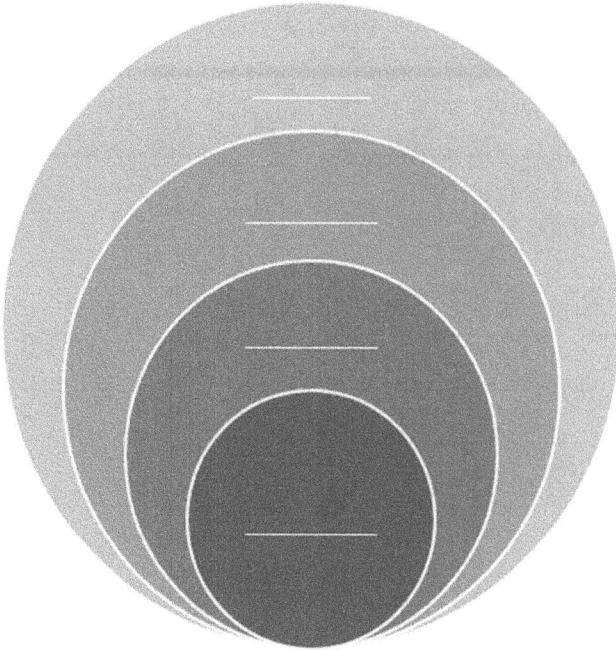

Get to the Root!

Along with understanding your core beliefs about yourself, look at your core beliefs in various areas of your life:

FAITH

- _____
- _____
- _____

MY PAST

- _____
- _____
- _____

CAREER/JOB

- _____
- _____
- _____

MY FUTURE

- _____
- _____
- _____

HEALTH

- _____
- _____
- _____

RELATIONSHIPS

- _____
- _____
- _____

FINANCES

- _____
- _____
- _____

Chapter 5

Get to the Root Part 2

"Sometimes our thoughts are backed with so much insecurity that they create lies we believe." — Unknown

As I have alluded to before, an unhealed person can damage good relationships, while a healed person influences relationships to blossom. At that time in my life, my core belief was "I am not enough." That belief manifested in how I interacted with my spouse. The following statements are my perceived thoughts and feelings. They are not a reflection on my spouse but truly a reflection on my distorted mindset that needed to heal. I believe I had to go through these trials to help others and to discover that my worth is not found in another person.

When I met my spouse in college. I did not realize it, but I was very broken. As we dated and got married, my brokenness became more prevalent. I went to several counseling sessions to help me understand why I felt so insecure in my husband's presence. He is the opposite of me. He has a big personality; he's loud, boisterous, a risk taker, and a lot of fun. According to the Marc Accetta Personality Test, my husband has a balanced personality and is able to co-mingle with anyone, while I am emotional and compassionate.[6] I always admired my spouse's strengths and resiliency. He can befriend anyone he meets. I am more reserved and like to warm up to folks. He is Yin and I am Yang.

> **TAKE A PERSONALITY TEST ONLINE TO GAIN MORE UNDERSTANDING OF YOUR PERSONALITY TYPE AND LEARN HOW IT RELATES TO OTHER TYPES.**

As a young wife, I always wanted to make my husband happy and keep him attracted to me. I wanted to be his number one. My desires were noble but out of order. (Side note: *Only God should be his number one.*) But because I had this deep longing to be wanted, I became a "Yes- woman." I never wanted to get in my husband's way as it related to his career goals and ambitions. Though I was supportive, I did not always like how things were panning out. I did not say much in fear of rocking the boat. Every time I remained silent in our marriage, a little piece of me chipped away.

> **SILENCE IN ANY RELATIONSHIP IS A RED FLAG. IT IS CANCEROUS AND WILL CAUSE THE RELATIONSHIP TO DISSOLVE.**

I was passive. Whatever he wanted, I went along with it. I did not ask a lot of questions. I felt small when I had ideas or a need. I literally needed things but found myself keeping my thoughts to myself. I rationalized my silence by saying to myself, "He works so hard for our family, don't disturb him." I was operating and relating to my spouse as a little girl. Little girls don't get married until they become mature. I often thought I needed to fix myself for my spouse to get his attention. I struggled immensely with low self-esteem. I had a deep longing for his approval, validation, and acceptance.

Because my husband is a social butterfly, I perceived his actions of connecting with others as a sign that I was not enough. I dressed the way he wanted, I fixed my hair the way he wanted, I even joined an elite group thinking it would draw us closer. I did not know who I was, and I was looking for myself in him.

I prayed daily for the Lord to change my spouse. But the Lord changed me instead. We often can pick out the wrong in other people so easily. We can identify their faults to a tee, but we are not able to see our own shortcomings. The Bible says, *"You hypocrite, first take the plank out of your own eye, and then you will see clearly to remove the speck from your brother's eye"* (Matthew 7:5). I blamed my spouse for my life being on pause. I thought that if my husband was more into his calling from God, our marriage would be better. I would advance in life, and I would feel better about myself. See, I thought the head of the house sets the tone for the marriage and the fulfillment of God's plan for the couple.

In prayer, God showed me that I am responsible for my life, my feelings, and my happiness. God never told me that I needed to wait on my spouse to live. We all have our own walks on this earth. My daily suffering with low self-esteem and confidence was my responsibility. My husband could not fix me.

My mood and insecurities drove a wedge in our marriage. I didn't trust him or other people. I questioned every relationship he had with a woman. It was taxing on us emotionally and mentally. I worried a lot about our future and wondered if we were going to make it. I was not okay, and neither was my husband. We looked good on the outside but were dying emotionally on the inside. I grew distant and blamed him for the lack of marital progression. I wanted to be my husband's best friend, but I wasn't my own best friend.

Do you see the pattern? All the things that I wanted my husband to be and give me, I needed to give to myself. I placed my happiness and fulfillment in the hands of another person. Because he did not know that I had those expectations of him, he did not meet my needs. I would say things to myself like, "I wish he would..." "I hope he..." "It would be nice if he..." "I would be happy if he..." So, when he did not fulfill them, I thought to myself, "He failed, and I must be unworthy of his love and attention."

Are you putting your happiness in the hands of another person? Are you expecting your kids, partner, job, car, house, money, or status to make you happy?

My husband tried to help me. He listened and walked many years with me through this web of insecurities. He suggested that I should just say what I needed. The problem was, I did not always know what I wanted. I knew I wanted to be confident and sure of myself. How could he make me feel sure about myself? He could not. He wasn't supposed to. If he could, that means he would also have the power to take it away.

I mentioned earlier that I joined an elite group for pure and impure motives. I thought this group would automatically make me confident and lady-like. I thought it would make my husband want to be around me. After joining, I realized that was not the case. But I got to the point in life where I wanted to be okay no matter what. I prayed to God for help.

The Lord sent a wise woman to speak to the core of my identity. She revealed that I went the other way when I joined that group. I knew I was not supposed to join, but I wanted to grow into a woman and be whole. I specifically remembered the day that I chose to go against God and do what I thought was best. It was an internal war of going back and forth with myself. I justified my reasoning and thought I had nothing to lose but a lot to gain. I was disobedient.

Have you ever done that? You knew you were not supposed to do something, but you became your own god thinking you know what is best for you? It is very costly.

God tries to save us from heartache and wilderness walks. He also gives us a free will – the power to decide which way to follow. I believe everyone will reach a point in life when they must choose between the plans of God and the plans they made up in their own heart. I did not think my choice was bad, but it was not God's plan, which made it bad for me. I knew it too. I sought several people about their opinion on whether I should join the group and if it went against my spiritual beliefs. That should have been a red flag for me. I was seeking approval and validation from people, but when my spirit spoke, that should have been the final word. I tried to rationalize with the Spirit. I tried to put the responsibility on God by saying, "If I don't get accepted or if I don't have the necessary money, then God blocked it and the answer was no for me." That didn't happen. God left the responsibility in my hand. I could have backed out at any time. I kept pursing something uncomfortably while broken. I was hurt in the game of life, but I tried to mask the pain, not realizing the damage.

This is how I ended up in the café with my hoodie on my head, hiding my tears. I realized I had everything – a husband, two kids, a business, a house, and two cars – but I was very unhappy. My pursuit of becoming a confident woman through an organization was not God's plan for me. Through this pursuit, my fear of being rejected was manifesting. I had several internal battles. You see, when you are broken it will show up in every area of your life. I wasn't supposed to rely on another external force to give me confidence. Note to self: Confidence does not come from anything or anyone.

When God revealed that I had sinned by disobeying my spirit, he gave me a chance to repent. I was so ready to heal that I had to walk away from this elite organization. I literally had to stop going to events and talking to members. It was very painful and hard. I did not want to, but I wanted to be okay. I did not want to be in opposition with my heavenly Father. It was slow and gradually faded. I was afraid to tell my spouse, but I knew that my life was in the palms of God. I did not want to disappoint him. However, my faith was anchored in God. Since I realigned myself with God, I relied on scriptures to help me when people asked me questions. I had to mentally coach myself through so many emotional times. I literally had to surrender everything that was keeping me from the will of God and keeping me from living my authentic self.

I had to journal daily. I had to meet with God daily to confess my sins and learn to hear God's voice over my own voice. I was in a season of wilderness walking. I was alone, on sabbatical from my private practice, and God led me to sit down from the praise dance ministry. I had to sit down and really acknowledge who was in charge. I had to learn that I could not serve two masters: I could not serve myself and God. I couldn't ask for God's plans to be done in my life while still trying to run my own life. In my case, God allowed me to have what I thought I needed. Yet he was waiting with his arms outstretched, welcoming me home. He was waiting to activate my confidence. It had been inside of me all alone.

God is so merciful that he allowed to me to confess my sin so I could get in right standing with him, to allow God to heal my heart to cultivate me into the woman I deeply sensed was there all this time.

Chapter 6
The Spiritual Roots

—————— · • ● • · ——————

"We're going to have to let truth scream louder to our souls than the lies that have infected us." — Beth Moore

I bet you are wondering, "We've heard all about the symptoms, how the roots of unhealthy patterns are planted, and the ways it manifests in our lives. Now, how do we heal?" This section will explain how I healed, with action steps you can take and apply to your daily life.

Counseling and coaching were my lifeline. I had a marriage counselor to help me work on how to relate and connect with my spouse. At first, I went to the marriage counselor asking her to fix me, because I thought I was the problem in our marriage. However, I learned that it was both me and my husband who needed to work on past issues within our marriage. We both had resentment, disconnection, and a lack of trust. We had to address very deep and painful issues.

Because of my insecurities, my husband shut down emotionally. He said he went into a vault. Due to my husband's actions, I became emotionally and physically distant. We got into ugly cycles and bad habits. My husband works throughout the day and long hours at night. I used to wait up for him, but he would work very late. I felt a sense of rejection and escapism in his working long hours. So, at night, I would go to bed earlier to avoid interacting with him. My coping skill from feeling rejection was avoidance. Since I was not getting my emotional needs met by my spouse, I channeled all my energy into church and our children. He was miserable, and so was I. I knew that if we did not get a counselor to help us confront our issues, we would eventually separate.

As I began to learn how to stop internalizing everything and improving myself mentally, my confidence started to take shape. Eventually, my husband joined me in marriage counseling. The first few sessions were rough. We both left the sessions upset. At one point, we started driving in separate cars so we could have time to reflect on the way home.

Marital counseling taught us to reflect on how we got to a place where we became two ships passing in the night. We were no longer lovers. My spouse was no longer my husband but my roommate. I remember our counselor said, "He is not your enemy." We had very intense conversations about our actions. My husband said he couldn't ever forgive me for my actions in the beginning of our relationship. I told him that if he doesn't, he will hold resentment for the rest of our relationship and we won't ever truly connect.

I was tired of appearing as if we had it all together. We wore fake masks in and outside of the house. I did not know him, and he did not really know me. I was seeking authenticity and eagerly wanting a quality relationship with my husband. The breaking point in counseling was when we had to decide if we were going to keep choosing each other or get a divorce. My husband was looking for an apartment, and I was calculating how to care for myself and the kids. It got real, y'all, but God.

After a while of processing our life, family, and faith, we chose each other. We chose to meet each other's needs, to actively listen, compromise, and date again. We learned how to do so with instructions from our counselor, open conversations, and role playing in sessions. In session, we each listed our top 10 needs and desires in a relationship, then compared our lists to assess our similarities and differences (see example below).

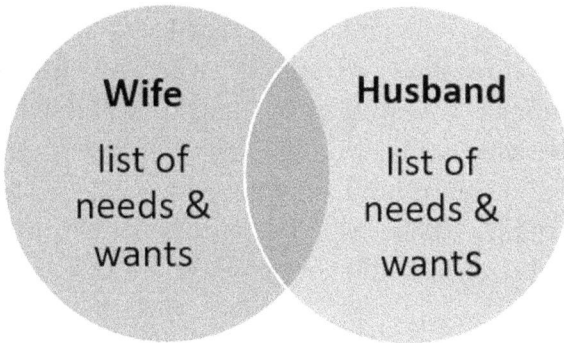

Wife

list of needs & wants

Husband

list of needs & wantS

To build trust within our relationship, we had to consistently share our feelings outside of counseling. We had to set boundaries that worked for us and forgive each other often. For instance, we had nightly check-ins where we shared about our day. We also had a bi-monthly date night, which helped us become friends again. Marriage exposes your strengths and weaknesses. Marital counseling taught us tips, tools, and strategies to improve our romantic relationship. Marital counseling is a process, but it is worth it.

If you are struggling in your romantic relationship, I encourage you to consult with a licensed marriage counselor to help get to the root of your relationship cycles and patterns. They say "insanity is doing the same thing the same way but expecting a different result." Stop being insane and change your approach by getting the right help. I know marriage is hard, but it is worth it. If you are experiencing domestic violence or physical or mental abuse, I encourage you to seek counseling and come up with a safety plan. Counseling is worth a try. It can save your marriage and family.

I also had an emotional midwife. She was a spiritual counselor; she gave me advice from a spiritual perspective and helped me see that my identity in Christ is eternal. She helped me identify the "Little Rachel" who was silent and seeking approval. Through conversations, she guided me through the stages of life and acknowledged how trauma had impacted my development. She was sent by God to help me understand that I can stand with or without a spouse. She helped me understand that I was first Rachel before I became a wife, mother, or business owner. Just like me, you are multi-dimensional. You wear many hats and fulfill several roles. You are more than a title, you are more than associates you are connected to, you are more than your past – you are fearfully and wonderfully made. I believe people will benefit from connecting with a spiritual counselor to activate who they really are.

She gave me assignments that forced me to talk with both parents about how I was raised and how certain childhood events formed "Little Rachel." Man, oh man, I was super nervous. She told me that if I didn't complete the assignments, Little Rachel would not grow up to fully operate as "Adult Rachel." I chose to do it afraid. When I talked to my parents individually, nothing magically happened, but subconsciously, "Little Rachel" was healing and no longer in charge of my life. "Adult Rachel" was feeling more confident and found her voice each time she completed an assignment. It was positively impacting my roles as a wife, mother, friend, and business owner. I became confident and willing to express what I needed and felt. I no longer felt small around my husband or like I had to please people to be accepted.

Each counselor supported me in different areas of my life. The duration varied depending on the intensity of the issues. After reading this book, you may realize you could benefit from talking to a coach or counselor. We are not to meant to do life alone, so getting support is wise. I understand that some cultures, families, and age groups are not in favor of sharing your business. I am familiar with the "what happens in our house, stays in our house" mentality. However, that mentality is more harmful than we can know. Some people suffer in silence, but they do not have to.

According to a United Nations report of 2020, "Around one third of women worldwide have experienced physical and/or sexual violence by an intimate partner; and 18% have experienced such violence in the past 12 months. Globally, an estimated 137 women are killed by their intimate partner or a family member every day."[7] I understand that people hope they are keeping their families safe by keeping secrets, but it does long-term damage to people's lives. Save yourself, save your family, and save your future. I am forever grateful for the support and wisdom that each counselor has given me to discover and home in on my individuality.

Get to the Root!

46

Chapter 7
Tools To Set You Free Part 1

————— • ● ● ● • —————

"So if the Son sets you free, you will be free indeed."
– John 8:36

Based on my personal and professional experiences, healing consists of three components: Spirituality, Theories, and Forward-Thinking Mindset. According to Strong's Concordance, "heal" means to cure, to make whole, and "to free from errors and sins, to bring about (one's) salvation."[8] For me to become the woman I strongly desired to be, I had to heal from the inside. All the external and material things do not equate to internal healing. I understand my purpose in life is to help heal the broken-hearted. I am called to set the captives free. To fulfill my purpose, I had to heal first. Spiritually, the Lord helped my unbelief in him first, then I was able to accept my position as a believer, and then I fully understood how salvation in Christ automatically activates my self-confidence. The way the Lord heals you may look different and feel different. Remember, you are so unique and special to God that your process will be specific to you. However it looks, trusts the process. Stay close to God, and he will direct your path.

In terms of theories, there are wonderful techniques and strategies that will foster inner healing. In my practice, I integrate various interventions such as Cognitive Behavioral Therapy, Dialectical Behavioral Therapy, and Separation Therapy. I will discuss how you can use each style of therapy to help you heal. Also, you must cultivate a Forward-Thinking Mindset. When you have been hurt or experienced trauma or abandonment, your perceptions become tainted. It is hard for people to think about their futures and to dream, create, and fulfill their goals. It is paramount that you actively have good vibes about your future.

"Sit at the Master's feet to get your healing."
- Rachel Logan

So far in this book, I have shared how prayer has birthed revelations from God. My faith is my anchor and has cultivated my identity as a woman, wife, and mother. I know that not every client of mine believes in Christ. Some of the people I work with are agnostic. I respect everyone's belief and accept that each person has a free will. I do not judge or pressure anyone to believe in Christ. In my practice, I acknowledge every client's spirituality that serves them. I don't want to offend anyone. I understand that my role as a counselor is to support and respect self-determinations. The Lord reminds me to love my neighbor as myself and to support each person along their journey.

Let me share my healing journey as it relates to my spiritual faith. My journey of healing with God started with me fully accepting and believing in God's words. I partially believed the word and what I heard at church, but for so long, I did not believe it applied to me. I had partial faith, only believing that the word applied to others. But the Lord increased my faith so I can receive power from the word of God. I read the Bible and learned the stories. One story increased my faith tremendously. It was a story about a father who asked Jesus to heal his son from an unclean spirit. The disciples were unable to remove the spirit, so Jesus stepped in. Jesus asked the father questions about the duration of the unclean spirit bothering the kid. The father said, "If you can do anything, have compassion on us and help us," and Jesus said, "'If you can'! All things are possible for one who believes." Immediately the father of the child cried out and said, "I believe; help my unbelief!" (Mark 9:22-24)

I was like the father. I believed, but Lord, help my doubt. I needed a renewed mind. I did not fully comprehend how prayer and faith can change my heart and mind. I needed help from Christ in my unbelief about my future. I thought my life was dependent on people and money. Doubt was the culprit, and I related to that scripture. I've been praying for many years for healing. I believe that my healing was postponed because I was unable to receive it by faith. A part of me did not think I could be made whole. I began to pray and ask God to help my unbelief in various ways in my life regularly. Whenever I noticed doubt or unease about the word applying to my life, I would say the words of Christ: "If you can!" (Side note: Imagine Christ looking at the father and me in utter doubt that someone would doubt him.)

As the Lord started increasing my faith to believe in him and his word for my life. I had to release all the things that were rooted in my life that were lies, fears, sins, and unhealed wounds. I had to let go of things that I thought were valuable. This part of activating my confidence was very vulnerable, yet awakening.

In my prayer times, I felt the need to confess my fears. I confessed all the fears I had about the world, my children, my family members, about dying, and about the longevity of my marriage. I literally laid it all out. I emptied my heart. All those fears were holding me back from living, and it was clouding my judgement. If you have hidden fears, expose them. Unconfronted fear can paralyze you, but when you expose fears, their false power lessens over you. I did not know I feared my children's future. I was a helicopter mom trying to prevent them from learning too many worldly things and trying to protect them from everything that is evil. I realized that when I was praying to God, I was praying from fear instead of faith. I prayed out of separation, not from a place of courage, power, and dominion.

As I took time to release fear to God, the stronghold it had on me was broken off. "A spiritual stronghold is a habitual pattern of thought, built into one's thought life. Satan and his minions want to capture the minds of people: the mind is the citadel of the soul. He who controls the mind controls a very strategic place! It can break off of you too."[9] Identify the patterns of thoughts you have that keep you trapped. Satan attacks your thought life. He is the father of lies and deceit. He purpose is to get you bound up in thoughts to keep you from moving forward. He wants you to think poorly of yourself. He wants you to second-guess your faith. He is your enemy. He does not want you to figure out your identity or how victorious you are. He is really afraid of the God in you.

People have several types of strongholds, and as you continuously connect with God, he will reveal your mental traps. Strongholds take root in your mind and penetrate the heart. Whatever is in your heart comes out through your actions. If you have realized that there are roots in your heart that manifest like prolonged sadness, anger, self-doubt, grief, or anxiety, you must destroy the stronghold with Christ. You can do all things through Christ who strengthens you (Philippians 4:13).

The first step is to acknowledge each and every thought that does not align with the word of God. I bet you are wondering, "How do I know what thoughts align with God?" I am glad you asked. It requires you to read the Bible to know how God thinks and to know his commandments. Become acquainted with the God-inspired words of the authors and research scriptures based on topics. Below is a list of strongholds and their meanings that you should become aware to cast them out of your life. As I am writing this book, I can relate to each stronghold and recall the times that

God has healed me from each one. If God can heal me, he can heal you too.

- Stronghold of Fear – Phobia. Feeling afraid, terrified, or scared that something bad is going to happen.

- Stronghold of Jealousy – Feeling envious, rivalry, spiteful, or coveting. Strongly desiring what someone else owns.

- Stronghold of Prejudice – "An opinion or judgment formed without due examination; prejudgment … reasoning that is self-based and therefore confused.[10]

- Stronghold of Popularity or Self-Centeredness – The state or condition of *strongly desiring* being liked, admired, or supported by many people.[11]

- Stronghold of Rejection – "To push aside, i.e., reject, forsake, fail; cast away (off), remove far away (off)."[12]

- Stronghold of Despair – To have no hope or a constant state of hopeless.

- Stronghold of Bitterness – Discontented, angry, greatly distressed.[13]

- Stronghold of Control – The power to influence or direct people's behavior or the course of events.

- Stronghold of Deceit – "The act of causing someone to accept as true or valid what is false or invalid."[14]

- Stronghold of Insecurity – "Deficient in assurance … not confident or sure."[15]

- Stronghold of Pride – "To inflate with self-conceit, high minded";[16] "deep pleasure or satisfaction derived from one's own achievements."[17]

This is not the entire list of strongholds that a person may struggle with, and you may or may not relate to this list. However, do not be deceived. Satan uses all these traps to keep you in shackles, self-sabotaging, and stuck. Satan shoots fire darts at you, and the word of God extinguishes every single one of them. Remember, strongholds are patterns of thoughts that keeps you bound. The way to get out of strongholds is to counteract each thought by declaring the word of God. Continual prayer and studying about this subject will give you spiritual knowledge and a great footing for your healing journey. Our fight for a sound mind and confidence is not with people, it is with the evil, dark, spiritual forces that want to paralyze you mentally so you won't live the life you really want.

I did not always recognize strongholds. They sounded like they were my own voice. You are not alone in the fight for peace of mind. Here are some examples of the trappings and the scriptures you can use to master them.

STRONGHOLD OF FEAR:

- "I do not feel comfortable leaving my kids with my family while my husband and I travel."

- "I am anxious."

- "I fear that something bad will happen while I am away."

- "I am constantly thinking about death or living in constant fear that someone close to me is going to die."

The opposite of fear is peace. Pursue peace. Peace is a state of being content, calm, and in controlled.

Scriptures:

2 Thessalonians 3:16 (NIV): *"Now may the Lord of peace himself give you peace at all times and in every way. The Lord be with all of you."*

Isaiah 26:3 (ESV): *"You keep him in perfect peace whose mind is stayed on you, because he trusts in you."*

2 Timothy 1:7 (NKJV): *"For God has not given us a spirit of fear, but of power and of love and of a sound mind."*

STRONGHOLD OF REJECTION:

- "I keep to myself."

- "I do not share my ideas with others."

- "I have surface-level relationships."

- "I feel like I am always being overlooked or never heard in group settings."

The opposite of rejection is acceptance. You are fully loved and accepted by the one who really matters. God loves and accepts you.

Scriptures:

Psalm 139:14 (TPT): *"I thank you, God, for making me so mysteriously complex! Everything you do is marvelously breathtaking. It simply amazes me to think about it! How thoroughly you know me, Lord!"*

Genesis 1:31a (AMP): *"God saw everything that He had made, and behold, it was very good and He validated it completely."*

John 3:16 (KJV): *"For God so loved the world, that he gave his only begotten Son, that whosoever believeth in him should not perish, but have everlasting life."*

Get to the Root!

STRONGHOLD OF JEALOUSY:

- "I think that someone is better than me, and I find myself not liking them."

- "I want what someone else has."

Jealousy turns into bitterness, and then it turns into anger if it is unchecked.

Scriptures:

1 Corinthians 13:4-5 (ESV): *"Love is patient and kind; love does not envy or boast; it is not arrogant or rude. It does not insist on its own way; it is not irritable or resentful."*

Genesis 4:7 (AMP): *"If you do well [believing Me and doing what is acceptable and pleasing to Me], will you not be accepted? And if you do not do well [but ignore My instruction], sin crouches at your door; its desire is for you [to overpower you], but you must master it."*

STRONGHOLD OF POPULARITY:

- "I want my name to be great."

- "I will do anything to get seen and get more likes."

- "I investigate how many likes I and other people get on social media."

- "I exalt myself over God or people."

The focus of this stronghold is being the center of attention. The trap is that if you aren't popular then you could be convinced to become "extra" by doing things that are outside the of your norm. The opposite of popularity is humility. Be meek or modest in your level of importance.

Scriptures:

James 4:10 (ESV): *"Humble yourselves before the Lord, and he will exalt you."*

Luke 14:11 (ESV): *"For everyone who exalts himself will be humbled, and he who humbles himself will be exalted."*

Philippians 2:3 (ESV): *"Do nothing from selfish ambition or conceit, but in humility count others more significant than yourselves."*

*STRONGHOLD OF PREJUDICE:

- "I do not like them because they do not believe in Christ."

- "I ridicule or mistreat people because of their race or nationality."

- "I belittle people if they are on the low end of the socioeconomic spectrum."

The opposite of prejudice is equality.

Scriptures:

Galatians 3:28 (ESV): *"There is neither Jew nor Greek, there is neither slave nor free, there is no male and female, for you are all one in Christ Jesus."*

THE ROOT CHECK-IN #5

Identify your strongholds. _____

_____

_____

_____

_____

_____

_____

_____

_____

_____

Combat every stronghold by declaring scriptures and/or affirmations. _____

_____

_____

_____

_____

_____

_____

_____

_____

_____

_____

Chapter 8
Tools to Set You Free Part 2

"My dark days made me strong. Or maybe I already was strong, and they made me prove it." – Emery Lord

There are additional ways you can improve your mental and emotional capacities. During my healing process, I used both spiritual and daily practices to overcome. There are hundreds of interventions and theories that professionals use during sessions. Personally, I integrate theories based on my clients' goals. I will share three practices that people can use to enhance themselves. I encourage you to research these practices by going to YouTube, Psychology Today, or other online resources to retrieve tips.

The first part of healing is your level of readiness. To experience positive change, a person should have acknowledged that something is wrong and have a desire to improve their life. If you are not ready to make changes, counseling or coaching can appear to be useless, when in fact, the individual is not ready to face the truth and make the necessary changes. So, be ready and willing to feel uncomfortable in order to become comfortable in your daily life. Become more aware of how mental and interpersonal issues are impacting your daily life. Begin to take heed to how your stronghold is affecting you in relationships, at work, at school, within organizations, and at home.

Practical or theoretical healing is similar to healing by faith. A person needs to confess their truth about their experiences. One way to make peace with your past to cultivate a fulfilling future is to write your narrative. Narrative writing is liberating because it encourages you to reflect on your life from an outer perspective. After you have, I suggest that you track your habit and use the Cognitive Behavioral Model (described below) to improve your mood and thought cycles.

Another option to improve your mental space is to become aware of your cycles. Cycles are habitual responses to similar events and triggers. Some cycles are healthy, and others are unhealthy. Some of people's behaviors are on autopilot. People find themselves doing things without being mentally or emotionally present, or reacting to certain things the same way each time. For instance, when my kids did not listen to me the first time, I would automatically become frustrated and agitated. Their lack of action triggered the Stronghold of Rejection, and I feared that they would be rebellious children. Being mindful of my triggers and emotions has helped me stop the old way of responding to my kids.

I use and teach my clients about Cognitive Behavioral Therapy, which was pioneered by Dr. Aaron T. Beck in 1960.[18] The goal with CBT is to help individuals rewire how they respond to situations. It also helps individuals manage their automatic thoughts. The old way of handling situations has expired. It is time to embrace a proven approach to stop unwanted behaviors and learn how to conjure up alternative ways to process events.

CBT is based on event, emotion, reaction, and outer-reaction. An event is something that you experience internally or externally. An event triggers or causes you to feel an emotion. Emotions are feelings that you experience in your heart or body as a psychological sensation, for example, fear, sadness, loneliness, contentment, or love. Emotions cause you to respond or react. For the sake of helping you get to the root, I want to distinguish between response and reaction. A response is a calculated decision to reply to an event or emotions, while a reaction is an impulsive reply to a situation. If a person repeatedly responds or reacts to triggers a certain way, it becomes a habit and an undesirable behavior. They become unhappy with how they are managing stress, life events, or day-to-day decision making. For instance, I didn't like how irritated I became when I would walk into a part of my house that was messy. Y'all, I went from a level 0 to 100 in 2.5 seconds. I do not like to see clutter or messes.

Typically, we focus on isolated parts of the CBT model. We say things like "I get so angry," "I hold in my feelings, then I blow up," "I think my partner does not love me anymore." Unconsciously, people can identify their thoughts, feelings, and response/behavior. Yet it takes intentionality to point them out before, during, and/or after a situation. This cycle happens in a split second, and it is easy to ignore all the signs that lead up to unwanted behaviors. Let's look at a non-fictional case and see if you can identify the problem, emotions, and reactions.

MARRIAGE EXAMPLE

A couple, Terrance and Monica, have been married for seven years. They have three children under the age of ten. Terrance works for an electric company, and he gets home around 6pm every night. Monica works full-time too, as a dental assistant. The family is busy with playdates, appointments, practices, and games during the week. At the end of the week, the couple is exhausted. Monica feels lonely in her marriage, and she has started in counseling to address this issue. She feels like Terrance is distant and does not have time for her. Monica gives him dry greetings when he comes home from work. She barely kisses. Terrance brushes off her attitude and shutdowns. He thinks she does not like him anymore. He wonders what is wrong with him. He covers up his feelings of rejection by watching television and coaching their son's football team.

From the Marriage Example above, identify the problem, emotions, and reactions.

THE PROBLEM IS:

MONICA'S EMOTIONS:

_____

_____

_____

_____

_____

_____

_____

MONICA'S REACTION:

_____

_____

_____

_____

_____

_____

_____

TERRANCE'S EMOTIONS:

_____
_____
_____
_____
_____
_____
_____

TERRANCE'S REACTION:

_____
_____
_____
_____
_____
_____

Now identify how Monica and Terrance could respond to their thoughts and emotions rationally.

MONICA'S RATIONAL RESPONSE:

_____
_____
_____
_____
_____
_____
_____

TERRANCE'S RATIONAL RESPONSE:

_____

_____

_____

_____

_____

_____

_____

In this scenario, the problem could be their lack of communication, intimacy, or their busy schedule. Each person thought their spouse did not want to be around them. They were both confused by one another's behaviors. Their emotional triggers were withdrawal, non-sensual kisses, isolation, and tension. When you can take a step back and acknowledge these three parts of the CBT, you can choose how to respond to situations rationally and with consideration that honors your needs or wants. For example, in this case, Monica could have responded rationally by sharing her feelings with her husband and expressing her desire to spend quality time with him before she started to withdraw emotionally. Terrance could have shared his heart by saying, "Monica, I am confused about your attitude lately. Is something bothering you?"

Whatever you think, you will feel, and however you feel causes a reaction. If you do not like how you are acting, check your feelings. If you do not like how you are feeling, check your thoughts. If you are troubled by the things you think to yourself, assess what has happened around you or to you. For every action, there is a reaction. Know the source of the pain to help you process your emotions to respond in a healthy and rational way.

I want you to practice using the CBT model daily until you get a hold of your cycles and responses. Use this model if you want to develop better habits, gain insight, and improve your mood. Remember, this model is a cycle. You can jump in at any point of the cycle to identify and gain clarity. You have the power to alter how you are perceiving situations.

THE ROOT CHECK-IN #6

Stop and truly take a moment to observe how you are feeling. What is happening in your environment, both internally and externally?

_____

_____

_____

_____

_____

Track your cycles for one week. Begin to see your patterns and rationally decide how you will respond in a way that aligns with your values.

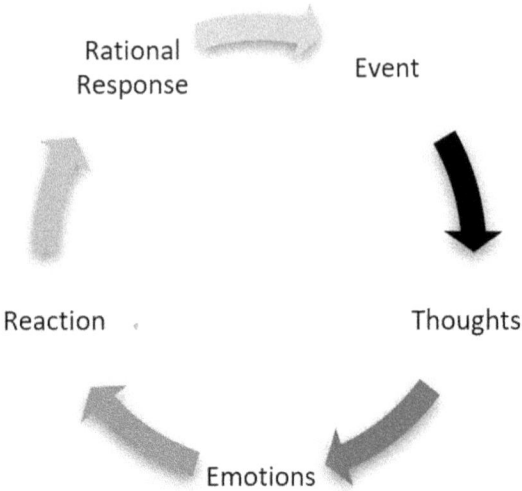

Rational Response → Event

↓

Reaction   Thoughts

Emotions

EVENT

_____

_____

_____

_____

_____

THOUGHTS

_____

_____

_____

_____

_____

EMOTIONS

_____

_____

_____

_____

_____

REACTION

_____

_____

_____

_____

_____

Rational Response

_____

_____

_____

_____

_____

Chapter 9
Maintain Your Healing

• • ● • •

"Recovery is not one and done. It is a lifelong journey that takes place one day, one step at a time." — Unknown

We have learned the power of Faith and CBT. There is one more aspect of healing, and it is possessing a Forward-Thinking Mindset or FTM. Cultivating an FTM actively shifts from focusing on the past to the present and beyond. It will help you discover the future that awaits. Frequently, we are more focused on what has happened to us versus what we are experiencing now. For instance, when I started dating my husband, I often saw him through the lens of my ex-partners who cheated on me with other women. I became suspicious when his behavior changed or when he started making new friends. Every woman became a threat instead of my friend. I was living in the past. Living in the past can cost you relationships, business opportunities, blessings, and joy.

To develop a strong FTM, it is important to oversee where your attention lies. Watch where your mind goes, so your feet will follow. I cultivate my FTM using pen and paper. I write and recite affirmations and scriptures. I found specific scriptures that strengthen my faith and renew my mind. I think about my goals and what I want my future to look like. I visualize myself in the future. I think about how I want to feel, my relationship goals, travel plans, business outcomes, and more. It is important that you capture your hope for the future. The past steals your precious time. I write my affirmations in a journal. I say them any time of the day, especially when I need a pick-me-up. I print them out and hang them in various places in my home. The old proverb is true: "Whatever a man thinks, so is he."

My FTM expanded as I read books and listen to podcasts on various subjects. Explore. Explore. Explore. There are new technologies, literature, and reports being released daily. I enjoy reading articles about different cultures and news around the world.

> **WHAT CAN YOU DO TO SHIFT TO AN FTM? HOW CAN YOU MAKE YOUR AFFIRMATIONS COME TO LIFE? DON'T JUST SAY THE POSITIVE QUOTES, BECOME THE QUOTES YOU DECLARE.**

FTM means having a bold, progressive, action-oriented quality state of mind. Assess if your current relationships, space, and other areas of your life qualify or match your FTM. FTM is an elevated level of viewing yourself and your world. People have to get on your level. It may require you to nicely leave some people where they are or establish a boundary if they are not ready to level up. For example, if a person keeps bringing up your past after you have healed from it, gently remind them that you have moved past that. If a person continuously compares the old you to the new you, tell them to get on your level. If a person jokingly references your mistakes, assertively remind them to get on your level. FTM blocks negativity in its traps. FTM is no longer friends with Complaining Carrie, Negative Nancy, and Gossiping Gloria.

FTM is ongoing. You are constantly changing; therefore, your mind and your will evolve too. Allow your heart to expand as well. What are you holding in your heart? Take a good look at what weights you are carrying. If old issues and pain are still running amok in your heart, how can you relate to others? With yourself? Are you holding grudges or resentments towards someone? How do you feel when you are around certain people who have hurt you?

Answer this question: To develop FTM, are you ready to condition your mind and heart to forgive those who have hurt you? If you said yes, start the process of learning how to forgive people who have hurt you so you can be free. Forgiveness does not mean you just forget what someone has done towards you. According to Robert Enright, the author of *8 Keys to Forgiveness*, forgiveness is the act of granting mercy to a person who has mistreated you.[19] Forgiveness is demonstrating love to a person who does not deserve it. He goes on to say that forgiveness grants mercy, and sometimes it can lead to reconciliation. It takes maturity to relinquish suppressed anger towards a person. It takes cultivating a willing heart and a strong desire to be free to see the person who hurt you as a human being and not as an enemy. It takes FTM to consider the place the person was in when they added a scar onto your heart and develop empathy towards that individual.

If you are a believer, it takes faith and supernatural grace from God to help you too. As believers, we are called to forgive those who hurt us, just like Jesus was called to forgive us of our sin. Jesus never sinned, but he was chosen by God to bear all our sins. Sometimes, you are called to be a bigger person to a person or group of people. You may be called not to bring up their transgression towards you anymore. God forgives our sins or wrongs in two miraculous ways. When we ask for forgiveness, he is just and forgives us by faith. God also blots out our sins and remembers them no more. To have FTM, we should have the mind of God and bring up people's injustice no more. Let God make your heart new to have crazy love and crazy mercy for people who don't deserve it. Vengeance is not for a believer, it is for the Lord. If you believe that God will fight your battles, he will handle those who hurt you. Rest assured that you are in good hands. Nothings slips past God's view. He got you covered! Forgiving others is not easy, but it is worth your peace.

Challenge yourself in the heat of the moment to shift, but whatever you do, keep moving forward. Keep pruning your thoughts to match your desired outcomes. At the end of this chapter, I will give you space to reflect and write your personal desires and affirmations. God can and will heal you if you ask him.

REVELATION OF MY AUTHENTIC SELF

I now know that my true identity is found in Christ, but I once thought my identity was because of the things that I have done. I thought that if I had the biggest house, if I had the best car, if my business was booming, if my husband was infatuated with me, if my kids were well behaved and smart, then my identity will be validated. My core beliefs were so far from the truth. I mentioned earlier in the book that our identity and self-esteem are cultivated in our primary years, as many therapists have recognized. I do believe that is true. But our internal identity, the one that will never fade, is found in Christ, and I had to really grasp that concept in faith. In Genesis, it talks about how God made everything, but after he made humans, he validated them. And I believe, just like in Genesis when God validated Adam and Eve, that when I was born and when you were born, we were validated. That validation is activated when we connect with him, when we read the Bible, when we grasp who we are spiritually. In my faith, we are supernatural.

The way that I really grasped this was through prayer. I lay prostrate on the ground. The Lord said, *"I love you. You are good. I made every part of you. I want you. You are special. The fear of rejection is a tactic. I made every part of you. Your mother birthed you, but I created you. I stitched you. I molded you and formed you. I have given you a godly identity, not a world identity. Not a title-based identity in your kids, husband, and career. Those things did not create or give you an identity. I gave it to you when I formed you in your mother's womb before time started. Your identity was there. You are good. You are complete, not incomplete. I saw all that I made, and it was very good."* My source of identity is Christ. I believed that my perception in identity being revealed my character will be formed. I am no longer subscribing to the identity of men, the world, my family, books, or people; I am only subscribing to my image of God. The Hebrew word translated as "image" in the Bible can also mean "shade," which means a trace, a shadow, resemblance, representative, imitation, being alike, serving as a symbol or portrayal.

As God began to renew my mind in my perception about my God-identity, he began to help me look at my other roles and identities. I struggled with my identity as a parent because there are so many influences that told me how you should raise your child. You have cultural norms, statistics, and articles. I mean, when you are a new mother, the world bombards you with so much literature on ways to raise your child.

All I really wanted, and still want, is to be a good mother and to raise responsible children who love Christ, who are intelligent, wise, independent, self-sufficient, and good moral people. In my struggle, I looked at other people to get a sense of how I should parent. I was even uncomfortable with my identity as a mother. I was feeling so uncomfortable during my outings with the kids. The reason I look to other women – white women, Indian women – is to get a sense of how I should be behaving. I was trying to emulate what I thought I should be, think like, act like, or do with my kids.

In chapter 4, I told you about a trip to a candy store with my kids. I took a picture of me and the kids when I was in the store. I felt extremely frustrated, irritated, and in no way well, but my picture appears as if I was calm, happy, and content, while on the inside, I was discombobulated. I need to walk in and operate in my God-image, not the system. I think culturally there may be helpful tips, but only God can establish the type of person I need to be for the people I am called to serve, even my family. He is my Creator.

Another identity that the Lord had me look at is my role as a wife. You see, I thought a wife was someone who was submissive and supportive of her spouse. I really got this understanding of it from Genesis when Adam and Eve were formed, and Eve was identified as his helpmate or helpmeet. I also got my sense of what a woman or wife should be from the Proverbs 31 scriptures. I often felt like I did not measure up. But what I've learned is that my identity as a wife is to help my spouse bring his vision to pass. I'm here to listen and to know the vision. Though his vision may not come from me or be like mine, it is my role to help him bring it forth.

So, I was somewhat interfering with my husband's vision because I didn't always agree with it, but I am not the visionary; God is. If I believe that my husband is a son of God, and he prays, I must believe him. I had to believe that his decisions were coming from God, and to believe in my husband, not question him. I needed to believe that God has his hand on our lives. As I've begun to understand and have clarity about my identity as a wife, I've grown to trust and accept my husband as being the head of the house. I began to truly trust God's whole flow and dynamic.

A double-minded person is unstable in all their ways (James 1:8). So, if I'm praying that God will be the head of my husband's life and I'm doubting the decisions that my husband is making, I am not trusting God. That is not faith; it is very toxic. My identity as a wife is not like my spouse. I learned that my identity is different from his because we are here to balance each other. We are opposites, and his strengths were made to counteract my weaknesses. Instead of looking at myself in a deficient way or saying, "I'm not like him, and he's nothing like me," I look at it in a positive way. We balance each other out. I wasn't made to be like him, and he wasn't made to be like me. We are both made in God's image and in his likeness.

There is freedom as you begin to explore your roles and your true identity. Your identity is not like anyone else; it is specific to you. As you take a good look at who you are and accept who you are, your strengths and your weaknesses, hopefully you will find confidence in who you are, because God does not make any mistakes.

ROUTINES, HABITS, AND COPING SKILLS

Another major aspect of becoming your authentic self is knowing who you are and what it is that you like to do. You see, some women struggle with this because they have spent a majority of their time looking after other people's lives. Women are caregivers, and so they find themselves in the position of meeting the needs of others before they meet their own needs. So, women find themselves burned out way faster than men. Women must begin to identify ways to meet their needs before burnout. Being an authentic person means caring for yourself way before you get to the point of frustration, irritation, isolation, anger, resentment, and bitterness. And you can do that by establishing consistent habits of self-care and utilizing healthy coping skills. Review the list of suggested copings in Appendix I for more examples.

It is stated that women are more likely to report feeling stressed compared to men; almost half the women in one survey stated that their stress level has increased over the past five years 32.

In the old days, men used to be hunters. They would engage in activities either individually or with other men. Women, on the other hand, were normally seamstresses or caregivers and did not have access to many recreational outlets. Think about it – there is a difference for women to find healthy outlets versus men. Either way, it is essential that you find healthy outlets that bring you relief, support, and love. It is also important to establish healthy personal goals and routines for yourself. It is better to plan and prepare yourself than it is to just let life hit you.

My husband and I had a thought-provoking conversation about how I could cope with stress other than eating chocolate. Eating too much chocolate causes my waistline to expand, and then I find myself trying to exercise to get the extra pounds off. So, in reality, overeating adds to my stress, and it becomes a never-ending cycle. So I asked him rhetorical questions: "What are my healthy outlets? How can I make chocolate, my current coping strategy, into my dessert that I enjoy after dinner?"

This is why it is important to have knowledge and access to healthy coping skills that you can use A) on a daily basis, B) during a crisis, and C) in case of a bad day. In Appendix A of this book, you will find a list of healthy, empowering coping skills derived from my personal family and friends. These are actual coping skills that people have confessed help them unwind from a hard day or improve their mood. I am saying to you that it is important that you create your own list based on what you need and when you need it.

Chocolate is no longer my coping skill. Instead, I have actively chosen to draw. I invested in myself and bought resources to help me improve my skill. For instance, I bought a sketchpad, pencils, and a how-to instructional book. It has brought me great joy to draw when I need to take a break or unwind. I have also actively chosen to research what my body needs. One of the coping skills that a family member suggested was eating high vibrational foods. I didn't even consider replacing chocolate with foods that elevate my mood and my body. As you are building your authentic life and disposition, it is imperative that you have tools and strategies that you will use to improve your life.

WHAT COPING SKILLS ARE YOU CHOOSING NOT TO USE ANYMORE BECAUSE THEY PERPETUATE A CYCLE OF DISTRESS?

ROOT CHECK-IN #7

My desire for you is to live this life as your authentic self. No fluff, no more "fake it till you make it." You can live with congruency in your thoughts, behavior, and purpose. Learn how to *acknowledge* your truth-past, *accept* the present, and take action towards a brighter and more abundant future.

$$Congruency + FTM = A\ confident\ person$$

Let's build congruency between your thoughts, feelings, and actions.

*Please note, I understand that you may or may not feel like you want to take all these steps, but I know you want congruency. A habit is built on a routine. The more you do something over and over, the more it will become a habit. Your desired action will become second nature to you.

Below is a sample of my steps to build congruency with my health.

Drink 4- 5 bottles of water daily

Eat a healthy breakfast daily

Take vitamins daily

*Drink a bottle when I wake up

*Drink a bottle between breakfast and lunch

*Drink a bottle with lunch

*Drink a bottle between lunch and dinner

*Drink a bottle with dinner

*Know my meal options for the week

*Oatmeal with fruit

*Boiled eggs/fruit

*Protein shake

* Eat after I drop off the kids at school

Take vitamins after breakfast

You can build congruency and consistency by writing your vision and habit stacking. Below, state your goal and write your desired action steps using the writing prompts: **HOW, WHEN,** and **WHERE.**

 _____    _____    _____

How:_____   How:_____   How:_____

_____   _____   _____

When:_____   When:_____   When:_____

_____   _____   _____

Where:_____   Where:_____   Where:_____

_____   _____   _____

 _____    _____    _____

How:_____   How:_____   How:_____

_____   _____   _____

When:_____   When:_____   When:_____

_____   _____   _____

Where:_____   Where:_____   Where:_____

_____   _____   _____

Another way to build your authentic self is to speak positively about yourself and your future. "Affirmation" comes from the Middle English word *affirmen*, and it means "to decide upon," "to state positively," "to make steady, strengthen," figuratively "to confirm, corroborate," and "to declare."[20]

Therefore, you must decide upon becoming your authentic self, and then position your mind and tongue to a state of positivity. It is a habitual practice to strengthen and make steady your renewed perception of yourself. You have to declare life-bearing words and then do what you say that aligns with your affirmations.

A sample of Rachel's Affirmations:

*I am healthy, whole, and healed.

*There is nothing wrong with me. I am fearfully and wonderfully made.

*I am more.

*I eat foods that give me energy.

*My space is clean and decluttered.

*I can establish healthy and loving relationships.

Now, take this time to visualize your future. What do you see happening in your love life, hobbies, finances, health, faith, career, family, and mental/emotional health? Write positive, action-oriented affirmations that will motivate you to FTM. For example, start your sentence with "I am," "My," or "I will." Stay away from phrases that start with "I am going to," "I should," or "When I... then I will." Write direct, short, and action-oriented phrases. Recite these as often as you need. You possess the power of life and death in your mouth. Speak life. FTM only!

Insert your name:_____'s Affirmations

*_____.

*_____.

*_____.

*_____.

*_____.

*_____.

*_____.

*_____.

*_____.

*_____.

Consider and write coping skills or a plan you will use to care for yourself <u>daily, during a crisis, and on a rough day</u>.

Daily Coping Skills	Hard Day Coping Skills	Crisis Coping Skills
• _____ • _____ • _____	• _____ • _____ • _____	• _____ • _____ • _____

Chapter 10

The Wrap-up

———— • ● • ————

"Our wounds are often the openings into the best and most beautiful part of us." – David Richo

We have talked about several concepts and reasons why a person experiences mental health issues, thinking scientifically, culturally, and medically. We have learned that in life, you could be Football Player A or B. Yet there is a third possibility: You could become Football Player C. Football Player C has finesse and adaptability. Player C experiences life's hard hits, jabs, and knee pain, but they address it immediately. Player C is consciously aware of how they felt before they entered the game, and they are aware if their equilibrium is off kilter. Player C quickly takes inventory of their life, processes recent events or plays, then makes a calculated decision on how to heal or bandage.

Become Player C and understand the significance of meeting your own emotional, physical, and mental needs. Dependency on people to fulfill you or make things better will only leave you thirsty and needy. Player C listens to their body and no longer ignores pain, headaches, or heartaches. Player C understands that their body is an alarm system that signals you when things are out of order. Become responsible for yourself. You are no longer waiting for the coach to put you in the game. If you did not already know, you are the star player in your game of life. At this point in the game, it is time for you to show up in spaces whole and healed. You have been called in your sphere of influences to do one thing. This is based on the concept of Sankofa, which means "it is not taboo to fetch what is at risk of being left behind."[21] Once you complete a level of your healing, go back and get someone who may be at risk of being left behind. Keep moving forward, but always reach back and help another person in the journey of life.

A generation consists of 30 years.[22] I believe that the reason we have generations is to give us time to experience life and learn from our mistakes, trauma, and mishaps to guide the next generation. By the time we bloom into our authentic selves, we can help those who are coming behind us. You release blessings or hardship. Each generation has its own style, themes, major world events, music, and revolutions. How will you contribute to your generation? Each generation needs its own deliverance. Come on, Player C, teach someone how to get a breakthrough.

Continue the cycle of life after you read this book and complete the journal promptings. Acknowledge your emotions and thoughts. Radically accept the things you can change and radically accept what you cannot alter. Take action that honors you, your faith, and your goals. Remember, building self-esteem starts with trusting your own voice. Respect your thoughts, wants, and feelings. Spend quality time with yourself and choices without judgment. Simply describe your wishes, perceptions, and ideas. Appreciate your ability to conceptualize your thoughts. Seek to know your truth before gathering opinions from other people. Validation starts from the inside, and confirmation comes from the outside. Get excited because you have a mind of your own. Self-validation is the secret sauce!

Be aware of devaluing yourself by engaging in unhealthy coping skills — you know, those self-sabotaging, camouflaged, unhealthy coping skills. Coach yourself to stay away from those long naps during your peak times and avoidance of hard tasks by working on something less challenging. Let's call it what it is... procrastination. Check in with yourself and dialogue via journal to see why you would consciously hurt yourself by allowing yourself to do things that go against your hopes, plans, or intentions.

Don't do things you really don't want to do. Do things with a cheerful heart. Recognize your availability or capacity without judgment. It is okay to say no. No one said you must run yourself down to be great. Even Jesus, the GOAT, took time away from his friends to rest. Rest. Take time to rejuvenate. Disconnect from the world. It amazes me how often Jesus left the crowd to commune with his Source. Let your breakthrough linger in spaces like a sweet perfume.

KEEP THE LIST OF UNWANTED TENDENCIES HANDY. CALL YOURSELF OUT IF OLD HABITS TRY TO CREEP BACK UP.

Use each season of your life to grow and to foster new dimensions of yourself. And if you feel like the book was a good start but you could use more support, join a Virtual Healing Circle. A VHC is a six-week group coaching session hosted by me. You will join other like-minded people who are ready to heal from the inside out. The group is based on the principles in this book. Virtual Healing Circles will empower and strengthen you to have congruency in your body, mind, and purpose. Come see for yourself.

ROOT CHECK-IN #8

Before we wrap up, what are you walking away with from this book?

_____

_____

_____

_____

_____

_____

_____

_____

_____

_____

_____

_____

_____

_____

_____

_____

_____

_____

Even though the book is over, continue your journey of getting to the root. Join the Healing Circle on social media platforms.

Appendix F
Coping Skills

———— • • ● • • ————

The following list of coping skills comes from my family and friends.

1. Ask for help

2. Watch funny or inspirational videos

3. Self-talk through the situation

4. Prayer

5. Write, then rewrite before responding when upset

6. Self-check-ins – reflect on how you are feeling and try to figure out why you feel what you feel

7. Read self-help books

8. Listen to music (good music can change your mood)

9. Yoga or stretching

10. Walking/Jogging or exercising

11. Admit that something is wrong

12. Talk to a trusted person

13. Therapy

14. Create and read Self-Affirmations

15. Eat high vibrational foods such as organic fruit and vegetables

16. Drink water (with fruit infused)

17. Drink tea

18. Deep breathing

19. Surround yourself with positive people

20. Go to lunch or dinner with good company

21. Retail therapy

22. Listen to podcasts

23. DIY projects

24. Light a fragrant candle to change the atmosphere

25. Ensure that you are in good health by a medical or functional doctor

26. Get yearly health exams: breast, dental, vision, physical

27. Take vitamins/supplements daily

28. Meditation

29. Soak in God's presence

30. Regular chiropractic adjustments

31. Regular massages

32. Evaluate your situation before talking to others

33. Take a soothing shower or bath with essential oils

34. Facials – keep your skin healthy and glowing

35. Paint your own nails or get a manicure/pedicure

36. Play with an animal

37. Research or read on new topics

38. Call 911 (only in a true emergency)

39. Chose to cope versus having a breakdown

40. Help others. Blessing others will bless you.

41. Speak out loud in a victory voice. It will awake your soul. Hearing your voice will get into your spirit and show up in your physical posture and walk.

42. Be still. Meditate on the Word of God and record anything that the Holy Spirit reveals.

43. Discover what scriptures say. Scriptures will build you up and remind you of what God says about you.

44. Dance

45. Get a mentor or coach

46. Admire nature

47. Write or rewrite your goals

48. Cook

49. Clean your space to brighten the energy in the room

50. Draw

51. Go on a spiritual fast to gain direction

52. Swim

53. Take selfies

54. Take a break

55. Join the Virtual Healing Circle

Endnotes

1.   Charles Whitfield, Healing the Child Within: Discovery and Recovery for Adult Children of Dysfunctional Families (Health Communications Incorporated, 1987).

2.   Diane Benoit, "Infant-Parent Attachment: Definition, Types, Antecedents, Measurement and Outcome," Paediatrics & Child Health 9, no. 8 (2004): 541–545, at 542–543.

3.   Healthwise Staff, "Suicidal Thoughts or Threats," last modified February 26, 2020, https://www.uofmhealth.org/health-library/suicd.

4.   Jessica Truschel, "Depression Definition and DSM-5 Diagnostic Criteria," last modified September 25, 2020, https://www.psycom.net/depression-definition-dsm-5-diagnostic-criteria/.

5.   David Prior, "Enmeshed Parents and Teens," Sunrise Residential Treatment Center, August 5, 2011, https://www.sunrisertc.com/enmeshed-parents-and-teens/.

6.   Marc Accetta, "Personality Test," https://marcaccetta.com/personality-test-2/.

7.   United Nations, "The World's Women 2020: Trends and Statistics," October 20, 2020, https://www.un.org/en/desa/world%E2%80%99s-women-2020.

8.   Strong's Concordance, "2390. iaomai," https://bibleapps.com/greek/2390.htm.

9.   "Pulling Down Strongholds: Strategies from Ancient and Modern Israel," 2000, https://www.lehigh.edu/~gdb0/simcha/strongho.htm.

10.   Bible Hub, "Prejudice," https://biblehub.com/topical/p/prejudice.htm.

11.   Lexico, "Popular," https://www.lexico.com/en/definition/popular.

12.   Strong's Concordance, "2186. zanach," https://biblehub.com/hebrew/2186.htm.

13.   Strong's Concordance, "4751. mar or marah," https://biblehub.com/hebrew/4751.htm.

14.   Merriam-Webster, "Deceit," https://www.merriam-webster.com/dictionary/deceit.

15.   Merriam-Webster, "Insecure," https://www.merriam-webster.com/dictionary/insecure.

16.   Strong's Concordance, "5187. tuphoó," https://biblehub.com/greek/5187.htm.

17.   Lexico, "Pride," https://www.lexico.com/en/definition/pride.

18.   Beck Institute, "History of Cognitive Behavior Therapy," https://beckinstitute.org/about-beck/history-of-cognitive-therapy/.

19.   Robert Enright, 8 Keys to Forgiveness (Norton Professional Books, 2015).

20.   Online Etymology Dictionary, "Affirm," https://www.etymonline.com/word/affirm.

21.   Carter G. Woodson Center, "The Power of Sankofa: Know History," https://www.berea.edu/cgwc/the-power-of-sankofa/.

22.   David Bayliss, "Generation," Bible Exposition, http://www.dabhand.org/Word%20Studies/Generation.htm.

23.   American Psychological Association, "Gender and Stress," 2012, https://www.apa.org/news/press/releases/stress/2010/gender-stress#:~:text=Women%20are%20more%20likely%20than%20men%20(28%20percent%20vs.,10%20(39%20percent)%20men.

www.ingramcontent.com/pod-product-compliance
Lightning Source LLC
Chambersburg PA
CBHW051432090426
42737CB00014B/2937